THIS BOOK BELONGS TO

A Little Book of

NAUGHTY
QUOTATIONS

JARROLD
PUBLISHING

A girl can wait for the right man to come along, but in the meantime that still doesn't mean she can't have fun with all the wrong ones.

CHER

I never jump into bed
with anyone straight away.
I usually wait
four or five minutes.

TARA SCHWARTZ

The only thing I regret about my past is the length of it. If I had to live my life again I'd make the same mistakes, only sooner.

TALLULAH BANKHEAD

NAVAL MANOEUVRES
Edwin Roberts 1840–1917

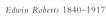

THE LOCK
Jean Honoré Fragonard 1732–1806

SEX APPEAL is fifty percent what you've got and
fifty percent what people think you've got.

SOPHIA LOREN

I once stayed in a sleazy hotel
where a stunning redhead kept
banging at my door. In the end I
had to get up and let her out.

DAVE GREENHEAD

*O*lder women are best because they
always think they may be doing it for the last time.

IAN FLEMING

*T*he best contraceptive is a glass of
cold water: not before or after, but instead.

ANON

*S*how business is like sex – you need
a good start and a big finish.

GEORGE BURNS

NEVER let a guy get away with kissing you on the
first date if you can get him to do more.

JOAN RIVERS

GIRLS AFTER THE BALL
Josef Borsos 1821–1883

THE ODALISQUE

François Boucher 1703–1770

*I*think nudity on the stage is disgusting, shameful and unpatriotic. But if I were twenty-two with a great body, it would be artistic, tasteful, patriotic and a progressive, religious experience.

SHELLEY WINTERS

The trouble with nude dancing is that not everything stops when the music does.

ROBERT HELPMANN

I'M NOT against half-naked girls – not as often as I'd like to be...

BENNY HILL

A lot of people complain about sex on the television, but
as long as you can avoid the aerial,
it's okay by me.

TARA SCHWARTZ

Better laid than never.

JOAN RIVERS

TOO MUCH of a good thing can be wonderful.

MAE WEST

THE BATHER SURPRISED

François Boucher 1703–1770

*M*y favourite mini-cab driver has a theory that tall people are good in bed because only they can reach the sex books that librarians insist on putting on the top shelves.

JILLY COOPER

Love thy neighbour is a great concept, but I always stop at foreplay.

TARA SCHWARTZ

CHASTITY is curable, if detected early.

ANON

Contraceptives should be used on every conceivable occasion.

SPIKE MILLIGAN

SHOW BUSINESS is like sex. When it's wonderful, it's wonderful. But when it isn't very good, it's still all right.

MAX WALL

My lover used to kiss me on the lips, but it's all over now.

TARA SCHWARTZ

AMORE OR LOVE AND PSYCHE
Antonio Canova 1757–1822

MAE WEST, *American actress and comedienne,*
1892–1980

I'll come and make love to you at five o'clock.
If I'm late, start without me.

TALLULAH BANKHEAD

*N*ever let yourself get tied down to housework if
you can get tied down to a bed instead.

JOAN RIVERS

I KNOW the difference between a good man and bad one,
but I haven't decided which I like better.

MAE WEST

A nymphomaniac is a woman as obsessed with sex as the average man.

MIGNON MCLAUGHLIN

It's often said that it's hard to keep a good man down; but it's sure fun trying.

TARA SCHWARTZ

THE GRASS is always greener on the other side of the fence. So if you don't want to stain your skirt, do it on this side.

JOAN RIVERS

A MALE NUDE
William Etty 1787–1849

DINNER WITH FRIENDS
Josef Engelhard, b.1869

What's a promiscuous person?
It's usually someone who is getting more sex than you are.

VICTOR LOWNES

When I'm good I'm very good,
but when I'm bad I'm better.

MAE WEST

I'VE FOUND the best way to keep my youth
is to chain him to the bed.

TARA SCHWARTZ

*D*on't ever make
the same mistake
twice – unless it pays.

MAE WEST

I‌f you aren't going all the way, why go at all?

JOE NAMATH

M‌y mother said it was simple to keep a man,
you must be a maid in the living room,
a cook in the kitchen and a whore in the bedroom.
I said I'd hire the first two and take care of the
bedroom bit.

JERRY HALL

THE CHEMISE REMOVED OR THE LADY UNDRESSING
Jean Honoré Fragonard 1732–1806

THE FIVE SENSES: TOUCH

Johann or Hans Von Aachen 1552–1616

$\mathcal{T}$he best distance between two points is cleavage.

ANON

I NEVER make love on
a wooden table.
It goes against the grain.

JACK YELTON

$\mathcal{W}$omen with 'pasts' interest men because
men hope that history will repeat itself.

MAE WEST

Agatha Christie has given more pleasure in bed than any other woman.

NANCY BANKS-SMITH

Two is company. Three is fifty dollars.

JOAN RIVERS

I once had a rose named after me and I was very flattered. But I was not pleased to read the description in the catalogue: no good in a bed, but fine up against a wall.

ELEANOR ROOSEVELT

BACCHANALI
Thomas Rowlandson 1756–182

AN ALLEGORY

Bronzino 1503–1572

*H*ell, if I'd jumped on all the dames
I'm supposed to have jumped on,
I'd have had no time to go fishing

CLARK GABLE

I'm into pop because I want to get rich,
get famous and get laid.

BOB GELDOF

A MAN is only as old as the woman he feels.

GROUCHO MARX

It must be admitted that the English
have sex on the brain, which is
a frightfully uncomfortable place
to have it.

MALCOLM MUGGERIDGE

As young girl I preferred to play
Dustman's Knock – it was similar to Postman's Knock
but dirtier.

BRENDA HARRIS

THE LEGS aren't so beautiful.
I just know what to do with them.

MARLENE DIETRICH

THE TEMPTRESSES BEFORE A WALL
COVERED WITH GRAFFITI
Felix Hippolyte Lucas 1854–1925

*N*eil Armstrong was the first man to walk on the moon. I am the first man to piss his pants on the moon.

BUZZ ALDRIN

To my embarrassment, I was born in bed with a lady.

WILSON MIZNER

Is it not strange that desire should so many years outlive performance?

WILLIAM SHAKESPEARE

THE SWING (LES HAZARDS HEUREUX
DE L'ESCARPOLETTE)
Jean Honoré Fragonard 1732–1806

*E*verything that goes up must come down.
But there comes a time when not everything
that's down can come up.

GEORGE BURNS

THE MODERN woman is aware of her environment and
always seeks to use renewable resources. That is why I
always date two men at the same time.

TARA SCHWARTZ

There are a number of mechanical devices which
increase sexual arousal, particularly in women. Chief among
these is the Mercedes-Benz 380SL convertible.

P. J. O'ROURKE

CUPID BENDING HIS BOW
Francesco (Mazzola) Parmigianino
1503–1540

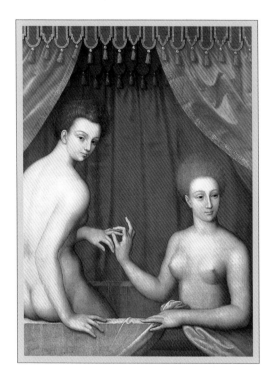

LADIES BATHING

School of Fontainbleau 1821–83

I was happy to be celibate for fifteen years, then I had my sixteenth birthday.

DAVE GREENHEAD

*B*etween two evils,
I always pick the one
I never tried before.

MAE WEST

I LIKE to play strip poker. It's one of the few times where the more you lose, the more you have to show for it.

TARA SCHWARTZ

GIRLS are like pianos.
When they're not upright,
they're grand.

BENNY HILL

How do I feel about men?
With my fingers.

CHER

Faint heart never won fair lay.

SARAH HARRISON

GERMAN EVE

Albrecht Dürer
1471–1528

IT'S ALL ANY reasonable child can expect if the dad is present at the conception.

JOE ORTON

There is nothing wrong with making love with the light on. Just make sure the car door is closed.

GEORGE BURNS

I wasn't kissing your daughter, sir – I was just whispering in her mouth.

CHICO MARX

THE STOLEN KISS
Jean Honoré Fragonard 1732–1806

Also in this series
Little Book of Humorous Quotations
Little Book of Wisdom
Little Book of Wit

Also available
William Shakespeare Quotations
Winston Churchill Quotations

First published in Great Britain in 1997 by
Jarrold Publishing Ltd
Whitefriars, Norwich NR3 1TR

Developed and produced by
The Bridgewater Book Company

Researched and edited by David Notley
Picture research by Vanessa Fletcher
Printed and bound in Belgium 1/97

Copyright © 1997 Jarrold Publishing Ltd

ISBN 0-7117-0982-3

Acknowledgements

Jarrold Publishing Ltd would like to thank all those who kindly gave permission to reproduce the words and visual material in this book; copyright holders have been identified where possible and we apologise for any inadvertent omissions.

We would particularly like to thank the following for the use of pictures:
The Bridgeman Art Library, Corbis-Bettmann/UPI, e. t. archive,
Fine Art Photographic.

Front Cover: *Angels*, after Raphael 1483–1520
(Fine Art Photographic)
Frontispiece: *Curiosity* (panel), Jean Honoré Fragonard 1732–1806
(Bridgeman Art Library)
Back Cover: *Amore or Love and Psyche*, Antonio Canova 1757–1822 (e.t. archive)